Great Kids Games

Great Kids Games

Lynette Silver

Sally Milner Publishing

First published in 1999 by
Sally Milner Publishing Pty Ltd
P.O. Box 2104
Bowral NSW 2576
Australia

© Lynette Silver, 1999

Illustrations by Jean Mulligan and Anna Warren
Design by Anna Warren, Warren Ventures, Sydney
Printed and bound in China

National Library of Australia Cataloguing-in-Publication entry:

   Silver, Lynette Ramsay, 1945- .
    Great kids games.

   ISBN 1 86351 233 0

   I. Amusements. 2. Games. I. Title.

   790.1922

Contents

Introduction

You don't need sophisticated equipment, specialised sports fields or even open areas to have fun playing games. No matter where you go, you'll see children organising games wherever there is a free space — in the war-torn streets of a city, in narrow back lanes of urban slums, in rural villages or, for the more fortunate, in private gardens or municipal parks.

The games in this book are universal favourites, and some have been around for far longer than anyone can remember. Because games have been adapted over the years to suit different times, places and players, there is no 'right' or 'wrong' way to play any game. Feel free to change the rules in any way you like. But if you do, make sure everyone playing with you agrees with them first!

Running Games

SOME WORDS YOU MAY NEED TO KNOW!

✳ In

You are 'in' when you are the person (or team) who has the first turn or who starts a game. This person is often called the leader and is usually the one who organised the game.

✳ Out

You are 'out' when your turn finishes for one particular round of a game. Players who are out must wait until the next round before being allowed to join in again.

✳ It

'It' is the name given to a person in a chasing game whose job is to catch the other players. 'It' can be identified by wearing a coloured armband or ribbon or by wearing a special cap.

Tipping

In chasing games, when 'It' touches the players' bodies, we say they are caught or 'tipped'. Tipping is also known as 'tagging' or 'tigging'.

Freezing

Players 'freeze' when they stop instantly and hold whatever pose they are in without moving at all.

Bar

'Bar' is a place in some games where people being chased go to be safe because 'It' is barred from going there. Bar may be anything handy: a tree, a wall, a rubbish bin, a rock or even a space scratched out on the ground. Occasionally, 'freezing' in a special pose can be bar. When players take up this pose, 'It' cannot tip them.

CHOOSING THE PLAYER TO BE 'IT'!

Nonsense Rhymes

The fastest and easiest way to choose 'It' before a game starts is for someone to volunteer for the job. However, although it takes longer, it is far more fun to use a nonsense rhyme. There are hundreds of rhymes, some of them dating back a century or more. Two well-known rhymes are printed here.

Inky, Pinky, Ponky
Inky, pinky, ponky
Daddy bought a donkey
Donkey died, Daddy cried
Inky, pinky, ponky.

Eeny, Meeny, Miney, Mo

Eeny, meeny, miney, mo,

Catch a monkey by the toe,

If it squeals let it go

Eeny, meeny, miney, mo.

You can add the following words to the end of the main rhyme if you want.

O-U-T spells out

And if I say you must go out

You must go out.

or

O-U-T spells out

And out you must go

If I say so.

WHAT TO DO

The players stand in a line or semi-circle with the leader in front. Keeping in time with the rhythm, the leader touches or points to each player as the other players chant the rhyme. If 'It' is to be decided quickly, the player being pointed to as the rhyme ends becomes 'It'. Otherwise, the rhyme is repeated with one player standing aside each time, until only one person is left. That person becomes 'It'.

Spuds

'Spuds' (a slang word for potatoes) is another rhyming game you can play to choose 'It'. As with many other rhymes, this one has been around for so long that no one knows where it came from.

One potato, two potato,

Three potato, four.

Five potato, six potato,

Seven potato, more.

WHAT TO DO

When the leader shouts 'spuds up', the other players hold out their fists (spuds), clenched and with the thumbs at the top. The leader, using a clenched fist, taps the first fist on the word 'one', the second on the word 'two', and so on. Each time the players chant the word 'potato', the leader taps his or her own fist to keep the rhythm.

On the word 'more' (the eighth spud to be tapped), the player puts that fist behind the back. The rhyme is then repeated, a spud being eliminated each time. When a player has lost both spuds, that player must stand aside. The last person left with a spud is 'It'.

GAMES TO PLAY

SAFETY FIRST

Choose open, grassy areas when you play running games. You'll need plenty of room to move about without crashing into other players or solid objects, such as lamp posts. Avoid hard, paved or concrete surfaces. They're hard on your hands and knees if you happen to fall. It's a good idea to wear non-slip sports shoes or, if the ground is soft and smooth, you might like to go barefoot.

Fly

This game involves both leaping and running.

What you need

- a long, grassy strip, about 2 m (2½ yds) wide
- 10 strong sticks about 30 cm (12 ins) long. We call these 'Fly Sticks'
- two or more players
- one player to be The Spider (the leader)
- one player to be The Fly

How to play

1. The Spider places the 10 sticks on the ground in a row. The distance between each stick should be either the length, or, to make the game harder, the width of one foot.

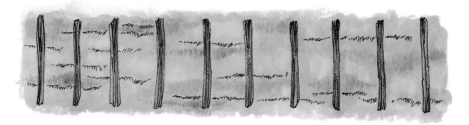

2. The Spider tiptoes between the sticks, taking care not to tread on them. If you tread on a stick you're out.

3. The other players follow one at a time. The Fly comes last.

4. When reaching the last space, The Fly leaps as far as possible over the last stick, stands on the spot and calls out the number of a stick between two and ten.

5. The Spider removes that stick and places it on the spot where The Fly landed. There should now be a row of sticks with a much larger space between the two. This completes the first round of the game.

6. The Spider begins the next round, making sure that only one

foot lands in the larger space. A player who takes more than one step in a space is out.

7. The other players follow in order. The Fly leaps over the end stick as before and calls for one of the sticks to be moved to a new position.

8. The game continues in the same way as the spaces between the sticks become larger with each round.

9. If The Spider is out, the next person in line takes over. If The Fly is out, the second-last player becomes The Fly.

10. When there is only one person left who is able to clear the sticks, that person wins and is The Fly for the next game.

Since The Fly can have any stick moved (except the first), some spaces may be quite large, while others may be very small. Having large and small spaces makes the game more interesting as well as more difficult. As the spaces get larger, the players will need to take a run to get up enough speed to clear them.

Crusts and Crumbs

What you need

* an open, grassy area with a Bar at each side
* two even teams, one to be Crusts and the other Crumbs
* a player who has a loud voice to be the leader

How to play

1. The players stand in the centre of the playing area, one behind each other in two teams, which are about 2 metres (2½ yds) apart. The Bars are at either side of the teams. The leader stands at the head of the two teams, facing the players.

2. The leader calls either 'Crusts' or 'Crumbs' in a very loud voice.

3. The players in the team whose name is called must run to the nearest Bar without being caught by the other team, which must chase them.

4. Players who are tipped join the other team.

5. The game continues in this way, with the leader drawing out the first part of 'cru—sts' or 'cru—mbs' for as long as possible to add to the suspense.

6. At the end of the time, or after a set number of games, the winning team is the biggest team.

What's the Time, Mr Wolf?

What you need

* an open grassy area with a Bar at one end
* a person to be Mr Wolf

How to play

1. The wolf begins at one end of the play area and walks along slowly while the other players follow as closely as they dare.

2. After they've taken a few steps, the players chant 'What's the time, Mr Wolf?'. The wolf, who does not turn around, keeps walking and answers in a gruff voice, 'Six o'clock', or any time he pleases.

3. The players continue to follow the wolf, asking the time again and again, until the wolf suddenly turns and yells, 'Dinner time'.

4. The players now turn and flee to the safety of Bar before the wolf can catch them.

5. The first player caught becomes the new wolf.

Variations of this game are played world-wide. In Egypt, children ask 'What are you doing, Mr Wolf?'. The wolf replies that he is brushing his fur, cleaning his teeth and so on, before turning with the yell, 'Chasing you!' or 'Eating dinner' — the signal for the players to run away.

Giant's Treasure

What you need

* a grassy area with a Bar at one end

* a player to be the giant

* something soft to be the treasure. This could be a cloth bag, an item of clothing, or anything similar

How to play

1. The players form a line across the Bar end of the play area. The giant stands at the opposite end facing away from them, with the treasure on the ground about 1 metre (1 yd) behind him.

2. The players begin to creep forward towards the treasure. At any time the giant may turn, hoping to see the players who are moving. If this happens, the giant points to these players, who must return to Bar and begin again. If the players think that the giant might turn, they freeze. When the giant turns his face away again, the players begin to creep forward once more.

3. The game continues until one player manages to get close enough to grab the treasure and run. When the giant realises that the treasure has been stolen, he turns and tries to tip as many players as possible as they run to Bar.

4. The player who is tipped first becomes the new giant.

Bull Rush

What you need

* an open, grassy area with a Bar at either end

* at least four or five players

* one player to be 'It'

How to play

1. 'It' stands in the centre of the playing area while the other players stand in a group at one of the Bars.

2. 'It' calls the name of one of the players. The named player must decide whether to run alone to the other Bar and risk being caught or to call on the other players for help.

3. If the named player thinks it impossible to outrun 'It', he or she asks for help by calling 'bull rush'. At the call, all the players leave Bar and run for the other end. 'It' is now free to chase and tip anyone.

4. The first person tipped becomes 'It'. However, if there is a large number of people playing, all those tipped join 'It' in the next game and help chase the others. As the games progress, more and more players become 'It' until all the players are caught.

Nose Bar

What you need

* an open, grassy area with the boundaries decided by the players
* at least five players
* one player to be 'It'

SPECIAL RULES

There is no normal Bar in this game. To be Bar or safe from 'It', players must freeze, hook one arm under one leg, hold the nose with finger and thumb and balance on the other leg. Players cannot be tipped while holding this pose unless they move. If they feel they will over-balance, they must run to avoid being tipped.

How to play

1. 'It' counts to five while the other players spread out within the playing area.

2. On the count of five, 'It' chases the rest and tries to tip one. Players must freeze in the Bar pose to avoid being tipped.

3. The first player tipped becomes 'It' and the game begins again.

Stuck in the Mud

What you need

- an open, grassy area with a Bar at either end
- five or more players
- one player to be 'It'

How to play

1. 'It' stands in the centre of the playing area, while the other players form a line at one Bar.

2. 'It' counts to three loudly. On 'three', the players must leave Bar and try to run past 'It' to the other Bar without being tipped.

3. Players must freeze with legs astride, as if stuck in gluggy mud, if they are tipped. They cannot rejoin the game until another player rescues them by crawling on hands and knees through stuck players' legs.

4. If 'It' is a good catcher, all players may end up stuck in the mud without anyone left to release them. When this happens, the first person tipped becomes 'It'. Otherwise, the first player to be tipped three times becomes 'It'.

Special rules

The rescuing player and the stuck-in-the-mud player cannot be tipped during the rescue.

'It' must not wait near a stuck player hoping to tip a rescuer. This is called 'doggy watching' and is not allowed.

BALL GAMES

· ·

The size of the ball you use in these games depends on the skill of the players. As a general rule, the more skilful the players, the smaller the ball.

SAFETY FIRST

When you play ball games, always use a ball which, if it hits a player, will not cause an injury. Never use a hard ball such as a cricket ball or a baseball.

GAMES YOU CAN PLAY IN AN OPEN SPACE

Poison Ball

What you need

* an open space
* a medium-sized rubber ball
* ten or more players, split into two teams

How to play

1. One team (the dodgers) stands inside a large circle formed by the other team (the throwers).

2. The throwers throw the ball underarm to one another across the circle, trying to hit the dodgers below the waist. The dodgers may jump into the air, duck down or turn their bodies to the side to try to avoid the ball, but they must not move from their positions.

3. If the ball hits a player fairly, that person is out.

4. To make this game more exciting, use more than one ball.

Countries

What you need

- an open space
- a tennis ball or small rubber ball
- at least five players
- one player to be 'It'

How to play

1. Players choose the name of a country.

2. The players stand around 'It', who throws the ball high into the air, shouts the name of a country and runs.

3. The players whose country is not called also run, while the named player (the catcher) tries to catch the ball.

4. The catcher yells 'stop' as soon as the ball is caught. This is a signal for everyone, including the catcher, to stand still. (If the ball was caught on the full, 'It' must restart the game.)

5. After selecting one of the players as a target, the catcher tries to hit that person on the legs with the ball. Targeted players may move their bodies, but not their feet, to try to dodge the ball. Catchers can reposition their feet as they take aim, but they must not move any closer to the target.

6. If the catcher is successful, the targeted player is 'It'. If not, the catcher becomes 'It'.

Tip Ball

What you need

- an open space
- any ball suitable for throwing
- at least three players
- one player to be 'It'.

How to play

1. The players stand in a circle with 'It' in the centre. If there are only three players, 'It' stands between two.

2. The players toss the ball to each other while 'It' tries to intercept the ball or tip the player holding it.

3. If 'It' catches the ball or tips the player, that person becomes 'It'.

GAMES PLAYED AGAINST A WALL

When you play this type of game, it's best to find a smooth brick, cement or stone wall with no windows. Make sure that there is enough room in front of the wall to play the game properly.

Foxtail

What you need

- a suitable wall
- an old stocking or a leg cut from a pair of pantihose
- a tennis ball or rubber ball.

How to play

1. Drop the ball into the toe of the stocking and then tie a knot to keep it there.

2. The player stands with the back against a wall, holding the open end of the stocking firmly in one hand.

3. The player chants the following rhyme and swings the ball from side to side or under the leg (every time the word 'Sir' is chanted) so that it hits the wall and bounces back.

R:. swing the stocking against the wall to the right of the player.

L: swing the stocking against the wall to the left of the player.

LEG: swing the stocking against the wall under the player's raised left leg.

Hello	*hello*	*hello*	*Sir*
(R)	**(L)**	**(R)**	**(LEG)**
Going	*to the*	*show*	*Sir?*
(R)	**(L)**	**(R)**	**(LEG)**
No	*Sir!*	*Why*	*Sir?*
(R)	**(LEG)**	**(R)**	**(LEG)**
Cause	*I've*	*got a cold*	*Sir*
(R)	**(L)**	**(R)**	**(LEG)**
Where'd you	*get the*	*cold*	*Sir?*
(R)	**(L)**	**(R)**	**(LEG)**
From the	*North*	*Pole*	*Sir*
(R)	**(L)**	**(R)**	**(LEG)**
What were	*you doing*	*there*	*Sir?*
(R)	**(L)**	**(R)**	**(LEG)**
Catching	*polar*	*bears*	*Sir*
(R)	**(L)**	**(R)**	**(LEG)**
How many	*did you*	*catch*	*Sir?*
(R)	**(L)**	**(R)**	**(LEG)**
One	*Sir*	*two*	*Sir*
(R)	**(LEG)**	**(R)**	**(LEG)**

and so on, up to ten.

All the	*rest were*	*dead*	*Sir!*
(R)	**(L)**	**(R)**	**(LEG)**

To play this game with a partner, the players stand side by side and hold one another around the waist. Chanting the rhyme, the players work as one — the player on the right swinging the stocking and the other raising the left leg.

Sevens

What you need

- a suitable wall with a smooth space in front of it so that the ball can bounce
- a tennis ball or a small rubber ball
- one or more players

Aim of the game

To complete the sequence without dropping or fumbling the ball. If this happens when there is only one player, the player must start again from the very beginning. If there are two or more players, the turn passes to the next player.

When it is the first player's next turn, play resumes where it left off.

Unless the rules allow the ball to bounce, you always catch it on the full. However, to make the game easier, players may agree to allow the ball to bounce before they catch it.

How to play

Level one: using both hands

1. **Sevens:** throw the ball at the wall and catch it. Do this seven times altogether.

2. **Sixes:** throw the ball at the wall, allow it to bounce once, and catch it. Do this six times altogether.

3. **Fives:** pat bounce the ball on the ground using alternate hands and catch it on the fifth bounce.

4. **Fours:** lift the right leg, throw the ball (underarm) at the wall with the right arm and catch it on the full. If you're left-handed, use the left leg and arm. Do this four times altogether.

5. **Threes:** throw the ball at the wall, but before catching it on the full, clap your hands together three times. Do this three times altogether.

6. **Twos:** throw the ball at the wall, but before catching it on the full, roll your hands around each other twice. Do this twice altogether.

7. **One:** throw the ball at the wall, but before catching it on the full, turn the body in a complete spin.

Level two: same as level one, using one hand only.

Level three: same as level one, using the other hand.

Level four: same as level one, with your eyes closed. This is very difficult!

Playing tip: Move well back and throw the ball high against the wall to allow enough time to perform the action before catching the ball.

Fum-Ball

What you need

- a suitable wall with an open space in front of it
- a ball
- at least three players
- one player to be the leader

How to play

1. The players spread out in a line facing the wall, about 1 metre (1 yd) apart and about 5 metres (6 yds) from it.

2. The leader throws the ball at the wall. One of the players catches it either on the full or after it bounces. If it is caught cleanly, the catcher throws it at the wall again for someone else to catch.

3. If the catcher fumbles the ball, that person must run to the wall and tip it before another player picks up the ball and throws it at the wall.

4. If the ball hits the wall before the catcher tips it, the catcher is out.

5. The game continues until one player is left.

War Ball

What you need

- a suitable wall for bouncing a ball, with an open space in front of it so that the ball can bounce
- a medium-sized rubber ball
- five or more players
- one player to be the leader (the King)

How to play

1. The players stand in a line facing the wall, about 5 metres (6 yds) from it and 1 metre (1 yd) apart.

2. The King, who is Number One, gives each player a number.

3. Using one hand, the King bounces the ball once on the ground and then hits it onto the wall on the full.

4. The ball rebounds with one bounce. Before it bounces a second time, player Number Two handballs it back to the wall on the full.

5. On the first bounce, player Number Three must handball it onto the wall, and so on.

6. If a player misses the bounce, doesn't hit the ball onto the wall on the full or fumbles the ball, that person must stand against the wall, facing the other players.

7. The next player restarts play, at the same time trying to hit the player standing at the wall.

8. The wall player dodges to avoid being hit and tries to catch the ball. Players must stay at the wall until they catch the ball.

GAMES USING A MARKED SPACE

Soccer Ball

What you need

* an open, grassy space with four bases (home base, base 1, 2 and 3) marked out in a diamond shape

* a soccer ball or large rubber ball

* two even teams, with at least five players in each team

How to play

1. Decide which team is to be in. This will be the kicking side. The other team will be the fielding side.

2. One player from the fielding side stands at each base, while the rest scatter around the playing area.

FIRST PLAYER (LEADER):

3. To start the game, the leader of the kicking side stands on the home base and kicks the ball as far as possible. The ball may be drop-kicked or kicked along the ground.

4. While the leader runs to base 1, the fielding side chases the ball and tries to kick or throw it to base 1 before the leader reaches it.

5. If the fielding side is successful, the leader is out. If not, the leader remains on base 1, or, if the kick has been a good one, runs to base 2, then 3, then home base. If running to any base is risky, the leader should not attempt to do so.

6. If the leader keeps running, the fielding side should throw ahead to the next base to try to get the leader out.

SECOND PLAYER:

7. The next player kicks the ball from the home base position and runs for base 1. The leader, if standing on this base, must run to base 2. If standing on base 2 or 3, the leader may choose whether or not to run to the next base. The fielding side may try to get out any player running between bases.

8. The game continues with each player having a turn as described above. A player standing on a base is only forced to run if the following player decides to run to that base.

SPECIAL RULES

If there are players on bases 1, 2 and 3 (called 'loaded bases'), all players must run. When this happens, the fielding side usually tries to get out the player running for the home base.

The teams change places when three players are out or when every player has had a turn, whichever comes first.

The team which scores the most home runs wins.

Hand Cricket

This game is a very simple version of normal cricket.

What you need

- a large grassy area
- two wickets (normal cricket wickets, wooden fruit boxes, rubbish bins) placed about 15-20 metres (20-25 yds) apart, in the centre of the playing area
- at least four players, divided into two equal teams (runners and fielders)
- a tennis ball or a rubber ball
- two players from the running side to be the opening runners (one at each wicket) and, from the fielding side, one player to be the bowler and one to be the wicket keeper. The remaining players are either runners or fielders.

How to play

1. The two opening runners take up their positions, one at each wicket, while the rest of their team waits to one side.

2. The bowler stands near one wicket and the keeper behind the other wicket, while the rest of the fielding side scatter around the playing area.

3. The bowler bowls either underarm or overarm to the first runner, who tries to hit the ball using one hand in place of a bat.

4. If the ball is hit, the runners must change ends by running and tipping the opposite wicket. While they are running, the fielding team gathers the ball as quickly as possible and tries to get them out (see Special Rules).

5. If the first runner reaches the other wicket without getting out, one run is scored.

6. If the ball has been hit a long way, the runners may decide to keep running to increase the score.

7. The game continues until one of the runners is out. A new runner then takes over.

8. When all the runners are out, the teams change sides.

SPECIAL RULES

The runner hitting the ball is out if:

> the runner misses the ball and it hits the wicket

> the runner misses the ball and the keeper catches it before it bounces

> the runner hits the ball and another player catches it on the full.

A runner is out if:

> a fielder tips a runner with the ball while the runners are between wickets

> a fielder throws the ball at a wicket and hits it before the player can tip it. This is called a 'run out'.

Skipping Games

All you need to play skipping games is a length of rope and two people to turn it, while another player skips. If there are only two players, you can tie one end of the rope to a tree, gatepost or fence at waist height. Then, one player turns the other end, allowing the remaining player to skip.

THE ROPE

Nylon, hemp or heavy cord all make good ropes. Your rope should be long enough so that when you turn it there is room for the player to skip and jump without bending over, but not so long that it is difficult to turn.

Players will find the rope easier to turn if there is a wooden handle or a large knot tied at each end.

TURNING A SINGLE ROPE
Normal turns

Turn the rope at a pace which allows the players to run in with the turn of the rope.

Over the Moon

Turn the rope at a pace which allows the players to run in *against* the turn of the rope.

Missing a Loop

In skipping games where one player follows the other, it is usual for the turners to allow at least one turn of the rope between players. This is called 'missing a loop'. In some games, missing a loop means that the player is out.

Keep the Kettle Boiling

Keep running in without missing a loop. If the leader calls 'keep the kettle boiling', players must run in without missing a turn of the rope.

Peppers

Turn the rope faster and faster so that the player jumps very fast indeed. You can use peppers to speed up the game.

Bluebells

As the turners swing the rope from side to side without turning it over, the player jumps over it. Depending on the game, you can swing the rope at a comfortable jumping height, very big and high, or very small and low. This is a good rhyme to chant:

Bluebells, cockle shells
Evy, Ivy, O-ver.

As the turners swing the rope back and forth, the player jumps over it in time with the rhyme — one jump for each word — until *O-ver*, when they turn the rope right over. If the player jumps the rope cleanly, you then repeat the rhyme and the game continues.

TURNING A DOUBLE ROPE

Use either two single ropes or a very long rope doubled. If using a doubled rope, one rope turner holds both ends while the other passes the rope around the small of the back and then holds the rope at either side of the waist.

Turn the two ropes alternately and towards each other so that they hit the ground without tangling. To avoid tripping, the player must jump the ropes alternately. When you use two ropes like this, it's called Double Dutch or Scissors.

OTHER RULES

Being 'out'

Players are out when they fail to jump the rope cleanly or, in some games, when they miss a loop. A player who is out usually takes a turn holding the end of the rope.

Deciding who will turn the rope

If no one wants to volunteer for this job, the fairest way to decide who will turn the rope is to use one of the nonsense rhymes on pages 11–12.

The players form a line with the leader or person organising the game standing in front. Keeping in time with the rhythm, the leader touches or points to each person as the others chant the rhyme. The person being pointed to when the rhyme finishes turns one end of the rope. The players go through the rhyme again to choose the other rope turner.

The rope turners do not have to hold the rope throughout the game. As soon as one of the players is out, that person takes over the job of turning the rope.

GAMES YOU CAN PLAY
Follow the Leader

This is the simplest skipping game there is. The better the leader's imagination, the more interesting the game will be.

What you need

- a single rope, turned at normal jumping pace
- one player to be the leader.

Aim of the game

To copy the leader's routine without getting out.

How to play

1. The leader runs in and performs any number or type of jumps, with or without actions. For example, the leader may jump high, low, with crossed feet or on one leg, with eyes closed, or may turn around.

2. When the routine is finished, the leader runs out.

3. After missing one loop (or more, if the players agree), the next player runs in, copying the leader's routine exactly. You are out if you don't follow the routine or if you don't jump the rope cleanly.

4. When everyone has had a turn, the leader goes to the end of the line and the next person becomes the leader.

In, Out, Over, Under

What you need

* a single rope turned at normal jumping pace
* one player to be the leader

What to do

1. The players begin chanting *In, out, over, under*, which is then repeated without stopping for as long as the game continues.

2. The leader may choose to:
    run in *with* the turn of the rope on the word 'in' and stay there for however long she wishes before running out on the word 'out'.

    run in *against* the turn of the rope (ie 'over the moon') on the word 'over' and stay there for as long as she wishes before running out on the word 'out'.

    run *under* the rope (ie run straight through the turning rope to the other side without jumping) on the word 'under'.

3. As soon as the leader runs out or fails to jump the rope cleanly, the next player runs in on the word 'in' or 'over' (or

under, if that person does not wish to jump). There should be no break between players.

Rivers

This game is a little different as the rope is wiggled on the ground instead of being turned in the normal way.

What you need

- a single rope
- one player to be the leader

How to play

1. The players holding the rope choose a topic, such as 'colours' or 'countries'. After announcing the topic to the other players, they then choose the name of an individual colour, country etc which they keep secret.

2. While the rope holders wiggle the rope along the ground, trying to make it as difficult as possible to jump over, the other players try to leap across it, at the same time calling out the name of a colour, country etc.

3. If the players manage to leap over the rope cleanly and not guess the secret name, they may have another turn. However, if a player is touched by the rope or guesses the name correctly, that person is out. If the name was guessed, the rope holders choose another secret name so that the game can continue.

4. The game goes on in this way until all the players are out.

All in Together Girls

As the name suggests, girls usually play this game!

What you need

- a single rope, turned at normal jumping pace
- at least five or six players

AIM OF THE GAME

Not to let the nanny-goat (the rope) flick the players' clothes as they run out.

How to play

1. While the rope is turning the players run in together and begin jumping, while chanting the rhyme. If running in together is too hard, the players may form a line along the rope and wait for it to turn over.

   All in together girls
   This fine wea-ther.
   I saw a nanny-goat
   Looking up my petticoat
   Woosh, Bang, Fire.

2. On the word 'Fire' the players all run out. Any player whose clothing is flicked up by the rope (this is supposed to be the nanny-goat looking up the petticoat) is out.

Room to Let

What you need

* a single rope, turned at normal jumping pace
* one player to be the landlord and another the lodger

AIM OF THE GAME

To complete your turn without getting out.

How to play

1. To begin the game the landlord and the lodger stand facing each other and start jumping when the rope turns. The landlord chants the following rhyme:

   Room to let, apply within
   The lodger upstairs is drinking gin.
   Drinking gin is a very bad thing
   So I will call a new one in.

2. While the lodger and the landlord keep jumping, the landlord calls the name of one of the waiting players. When the named player runs in to answer the call, the lodger (who is being

evicted) must run out. The landlord must keep jumping while this is happening. If a player does not jump the rope properly or fails to run in or out cleanly, that person becomes a rope turner.

3. When all the players have had a turn at being the lodger, a new landlord is chosen and the game starts again.

Postman, Postman

This game can be played by just two people — one person skipping with an individual rope and the other running in.

What you need

* a single rope, turned at normal jumping pace

* one player to jump and another to run in.

How to play

1. The first player begins jumping and chants

    Postman, postman

    Knocking at the door.

    In comes (the jumper calls another player's name) *from next door.*

2. While the rope keeps turning the named person runs in and joins the first player. They jump together as the rhyme continues

    How many letters did you bring?

    One, two, three, four, etc.

3. The two players continue jumping until one of them fails to jump the rope cleanly. The number on which the rope stops is the number of letters delivered. To speed up the game, peppers may be turned when the counting begins.

H-E-L-P-W-BB

What you need

* a single rope, turned at normal jumping pace
* one player to be the leader

How to play

1. While the rest of the players chant the letters *H E L P W BB* — one letter for each turn of the rope — the leader runs in and begins jumping. If the leader is not out after the players chant the letters twice, the turners turn the rope faster.

2. If the rope stops on the letter

H: the leader continues jumping for as long as possible while the turners turn the rope high above the ground.

E: the leader continues jumping with eyes closed.

L: the leader continues jumping in a crouched position while the turners turn the rope very low.

P: the leader continues jumping while the rope turns peppers.

W: the leader continues jumping while the turners wriggle the rope like a snake, starting at ground-level and gradually rising.

BB: the leader continues jumping bluebells while the others chant the bluebell rhyme (see page 38).

3. When the leader is out performing the special jumps, the next player has a turn.

Down the Mississippi

What you need

* a single rope, turned at normal jumping pace
* one player to be the leader

AIM OF THE GAME

To 'keep the kettle boiling'. Any player who misses a loop is out.

How to play

1. While the others chant:
    *Down **the Mississippi** if **you** miss **the loop you're** out,*
    the leader runs in on the word ***down*** and begins jumping, one
    jump on each syllable printed in dark type.

2. On the word ***out***, the leader runs out and the players repeat the
    rhyme without a pause. The next player must run in
    immediately and begin jumping on the word ***down***. If a loop is
    missed, the player is out.

3. The game continues until there are only two players left. Then
    a new game can begin.

Teddy Bear

What you need

*   a single rope, turned at normal jumping pace
*   one player to be the leader

Aim of the game

To complete the entire rhyme without getting out.

How to play

1. The leader runs in and jumps the rope, doing the actions given
    in brackets while the others chant the following rhyme:

    Teddy Bear, Teddy Bear (normal jumps)
    Turn a-round (player turns 180° to face the other way)
    Teddy Bear, Teddy Bear (normal jumps)
    Touch the ground (player touches the ground with one hand)

    Teddy Bear, Teddy Bear (normal jumps)
    Climb the stair (player moves hands in the air as if climbing a
    ladder)

    Teddy Bear, Teddy Bear (normal jumps)
    Say your prayers (player puts hands together as if praying and
    closes eyes)

Teddy Bear, Teddy Bear (normal jumps)
Turn off the light (player lifts a hand as if turning off a light)

Teddy Bear, Teddy Bear (normal jumps)
Say goodnight (player blows a kiss and runs out).

2. The game continues until all players have had a turn.

Figure Eights

What you need

✻ a single rope, turned at normal jumping pace

✻ one player to be the leader

AIM OF THE GAME

Not to miss a loop

How to play

1. The players follow the leader by running in, jumping the rope once and running out without missing a loop.

2. Players who miss a loop are out.

3. When two players are left, the game restarts.

4.   The leader may perform actions with each jump to make the game more difficult.

Alphabet Skip

What you need

* a single rope, turned at normal jumping pace
* one player to be the leader

AIM OF THE GAME

No one is ever out in this game. Instead of being out when the rope stops, the player gets an answer to questions. Take care not to giggle too much or you might not be able to jump properly!

How to play

1.   The leader runs in and begins jumping while the others chant the alphabet, one letter for each turn of the rope.

2.   If the leader hasn't missed a jump by the time the chant reaches Z, the players repeat the alphabet and turn the rope faster and faster, until the leader misses.

3.   The leader chooses a name belonging to the opposite sex which begins with the letter on which the rope stopped. In the following example, the rope has stopped on the letter S, so the leader, who is a girl, has chosen a boy's name, Scott.

4.   The leader starts jumping again while the players chant: *Scott Scott come to tea, Scott Scott marry me,* followed by *Yes/No* which is repeated (with peppers if necessary) until the rope stops.

5.   If the rope stopped on *no,* the next player has a turn.

6.   If the rope stopped on *yes,* the players chant: *Where will we be married?* followed by *Church, garden, toilet?* which is repeated, using peppers if necessary, until an answer is obtained.

7.   *How many children will we have?* followed by *one, two, three, four?* etc. After number ten, use peppers to get an answer.

8. *How many dirty nap-pies?* followed by *one, two* etc, as above.

9. *How many bottles will there be?* followed by *one, two* etc, as above.

10. The rhyme is now complete.

Jelly on the Plate

What you need

* a single rope, turned at normal jumping speed
* one player to be the leader

AIM OF THE GAME

To complete the rhyme without getting out

How to play

1. The leader runs in and begins performing the actions given in the brackets while the others chant.

   Jelly on the plate, jelly on the plate (normal jumps)
   Wibble wobble, wibble wobble (while jumping, wobble the hips)
   Jelly on the plate (normal jumps)

   Sausage in the pan, sausage in the pan (normal jumps)
   Turn it over, turn it over (turn around while jumping)
   Sausage in the pan (normal jumps)

   Jam on the shelf, jam on the shelf (normal jumps)
   Get it down, get it down (while jumping, reach above head with one arm as if getting jam from a high shelf)
   Jam on the shelf (normal jumps)

   Money on the ground, money on the ground (normal jumps)
   Pick it up, pick it up (while jumping, touch the ground with a hand as if picking up coins)
   Money on the ground (normal jumps)

Dirt on the floor, dirt on the floor (normal jumps)

Sweep it up, sweep it up (while jumping, brush the ground with a hand as if sweeping)

Dirt on the floor (normal jumps)

Robbers in the house, robbers in the house (normal jumps)

Kick them out, kick them out (while jumping, kick one leg)

Robbers in the house (normal jumps)

Apples on the tree, apples on the tree (normal jumps)

Pick them off, pick them off (while jumping, reach up as if picking apples from a tree)

Apples on the tree (normal jumps)

Ants in your pants, ants in your pants (normal jumps)

Get them out, get them out (while jumping, frantically scratch the clothing)

Ants in your pants (normal jumps)

2. If a player fails to jump the rope cleanly or perform the actions properly, the next player has a turn.

Christopher Columbus

What you need

* a single rope, swung according to the rhyme
* one player to be the leader

AIM OF THE GAME

This is a difficult action rhyme game which each player tries to complete. If the player fails to clear the rope or cannot perform the actions, the next person gets a turn.

How to play

1. While the leader jumps and does the actions given in the brackets, the other players chant:

Christopher Columbus sailed the seven seas (normal bluebells)
The waves got higher (larger bluebells)
The waves got bigger (very large bluebells)
The waves turned over (jump as the rope turns over)
Christopher Columbus lost an arm (jump the turned rope with one arm behind back)

Christopher Columbus lost the other arm (jump the turned rope with two arms behind back)

Christopher Columbus lost a leg (hop on one leg over the turned rope, with arms still behind back)

Christopher Columbus lost an eye (hop on one leg over turned rope, arms behind back, one eye closed)

Christopher Columbus lost the other eye (hop on one leg over turned rope, arms behind back, both eyes closed)

Christopher Columbus hit his head (hop on one leg over the turned rope, hands behind back, both eyes closed and head hanging down)

Christopher Columbus fell down dead (jump over the turned rope and then run out on the word dead).

Elastics

Although elastics is only a recent game compared to many others, its popularity in countries where it is played is enormous. Like many of the skipping games, it also has a rhyme which is chanted as the players work their way through the game.

WHAT YOU NEED

⁕ a piece of elastic at least 6 mm (¼") wide and about 4 metres (3¾ yards) long, with the ends tied firmly together

⁕ any flat playing surface, either indoors or out

⁕ at least three players, two to stretch the elastic (the holders) and one to jump. For Level 3, three holders are needed.

Deciding who will be the holders

If no one volunteers for this job, the holders can be chosen by using one of the nonsense rhymes on page 11.

THE RHYME

England, Ireland, Scotland, Wales

Inside, Outside, Inside, Scales.

(For feet positions when chanting this rhyme, see below)

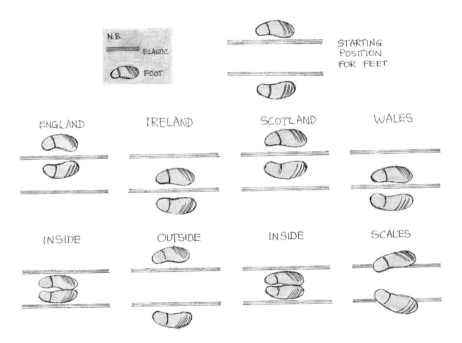

Aim of the game

To complete the routine without getting out. You will notice that the elastic is raised in height as the game progresses, so that each level is a little more difficult than the previous one. The levels are called Ankles, Hips, Waists, Under Arms, Neck and Sky High.

How to play

While chanting the rhyme, the players work their way through the levels until they are out. When players are out they must wait until their next turn, when they resume where they left off.

Being out

If the player is unable to do any routine according to the special rules for each level, that person is out and the turn passes to the next player.

GAMES TO PLAY

Level One – Normal width

Ankles

* The holders stand facing one another. After passing the elastic around their ankles, they stand with their feet slightly apart and move away from one another until the elastic is lightly stretched, but still has plenty of bounce.

The first player then takes up the starting position (see page 55).

* While the others chant the rhyme, the first player begins jumping over the elastic, making sure that the feet are in the positions shown on the page 55.

SPECIAL RULES

- the jumps must be clean
- the feet must land on the elastic on the word 'scales'

Knees

This is the same as Ankles, except that the holders raise the elastic to knee height.

Special Rules

* the player must continue to jump cleanly
* the player must not touch or push down the elastic with the hands
* the feet must land on the elastic on the word 'scales'

THERE ARE SLIGHT CHANGES TO THE ROUTINE AND RULES FROM NOW ON.

With the elastic being raised higher from the ground, the player no longer jumps but switches to a scissors dance. This is a high scissors kick over the elastic with one leg, followed by a hopping rebound, followed by another high kick over the elastic with the other leg.

SPECIAL RULES

✳   On the word 'scales', instead of standing on the elastic, the player's feet return to the starting position. (See page 55.)

✳   The player's legs may touch the elastic.

✳   Where allowed (in Under Arms, Necks and Sky High), the tip of the little finger may be used to lower the elastic.

✳   The rhythm must be maintained throughout the scissors dance. If it is lost, the player is out.

Hips

For Hips the elastic is raised so that it is just under the holders' bottoms.

The players perform the routine using the scissors dance but must not lower the elastic with their hands.

Waists

The holders raise the elastic to waist level, forcing the jumper to do an even higher scissors dance. This is very difficult. Although the legs can touch the elastic, the player must still perform the routine without any assistance from the hands.

Under Arms

With the elastic raised so that it is under the armpits of the holders, the player may now use the smallest finger on either hand to pull the elastic down so that the routine can be completed using the scissors dance.

Necks

This is the same as Under Arms except that the elastic is now around the necks of the holders.

Sky High

Using their hands, the holders raise the elastic high above their heads. The player completes the routine with a scissors dance as before, again using the little finger to pull the elastic down.

Level Two – Skinnies

The routine is exactly the same as that given for Level 1.

However, to make it harder, the width of the jumping area is reduced.

To do this, the holders stand apart as before but pass the elastic around one leg only (for Ankles, Knees and Hips) and around two arms held closely together and at the appropriate height (for Waists, Under Arms, Necks and Sky High).

Level Three — Triangles

The routine now changes, with three holders forming a triangle with the elastic, as shown below.

The player performs the new routine, with the elastic being raised Knees, Hips etc as before, following the feet patterns shown below.

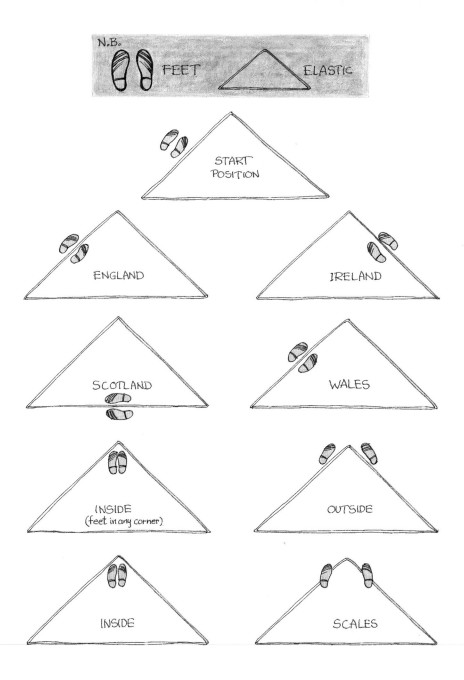

N.B.   FEET   ELASTIC

START POSITION

ENGLAND

IRELAND

SCOTLAND

WALES

INSIDE
(feet in any corner)

OUTSIDE

INSIDE

SCALES

Level Four – Wides

Level 4 needs two holders and the routine is the same as that for Levels 1 and 2 except that the elastic is held wide apart.

For Ankles, Knees and Hips, the holders stand with their legs as far apart as possible.

For Waists, Under Arms, Necks and Sky High, they hold the elastic apart with their hands.

Marbles

Marbles, which is rather like mini-bowls, is an ancient game. Once played by Roman soldiers and American Indians, marbles has been so popular over the years that it's still alive and well in modern times! Although nowadays players use balls made of glass, about 300 years ago balls made from marble came into fashion. These replaced the clay balls, nuts and round pebbles previously used and gave the game its name.

CHOOSING A PLACE TO PLAY

The best place to play marbles is on bare dirt, although the players may end up looking a little grubby by the end of the game. If you do play the game on dirt, use a stick to draw any lines you need. If you use a paved surface, keep some chalk or a crayon handy.

If there are obstacles in the playing area, such as twigs, rocks, or lumps of earth, you should decide whether to clear these away before the game begins. In some games, it is more fun if you have to avoid the obstacles!

BEFORE YOU BEGIN

Taw or shooter

This is the marble which does all the work when playing. Most players have a favourite marble which they always use as the taw.

Shooting

Shooting is trying to hit another player's marble with the taw. Here are some of the ways you can do this.

Rolling: this is best for beginners as all the player has to do is roll the taw along the ground.

Flicking: a quick flick with the index finger is especially useful when trying to hit a very close target.

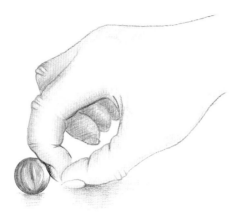

Squeezing: hold the marble between the thumb and index finger and squeeze it.

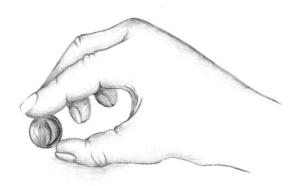

Knuckling: good marble players generally use this method. Rest the knuckles of the shooting hand on the ground, bend in the thumb and place the taw in the crook of the first or second finger. Shoot the taw by flicking the thumb forward.

Shooting line

In some games the players shoot from behind a line. This is called the shooting line.

Fudging

'Fudging' is when you let your hand creep over the shooting line while you are playing. This is not allowed and players who fudge face a penalty, such as having the shoot disallowed or missing the turn completely.

Playing for keeps

Before beginning any game, players must decide if they will keep any marbles they win. If you play for keeps, make sure that you do not use your favourite marbles!

GAMES PLAYED IN A RING

Most ring games need a circle and a shooting line. To decide who goes first, each player shoots a taw from behind a shooting line towards the circle. The player whose taw goes closest, but not into the circle, has the first turn.

Target

What you need

- four circles marked on the ground, one inside the other, with the one in the centre about ten centimetres (4 inches) in diameter. The circles should be about five centimetres (2 inches) apart. The inner circle is worth fifty points, the next twenty, the next ten and the last one, five points.

- a shooting line, drawn about two metres (6 feet) away from the outer circle.

- three marbles for each player.

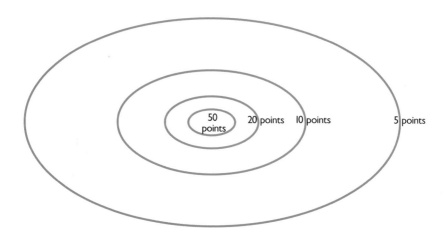

AIM OF THE GAME

To get the highest score

How to Play

TWO OR MORE PLAYERS

1. The first player shoots three marbles onto the target, adds up the score and removes the marbles. If a marble lands on a line, the lower score is counted.

2. The next player has a turn.

3. After an agreed number of rounds, the player with the highest score at the end of the game is the winner.

TWO PLAYERS ONLY

1. The first player shoots three marbles but does not remove them from the target.

2. The next player shoots three marbles, trying to knock the first player's marbles off the target.

3. The scores are added up.

4. The game continues with the players taking turns at being first.

5. At the end of the game, the player with the highest score wins.

In a ring

What you need

- a circle about a metre (3 feet) in diameter
- a shooting line about two metres (6 feet) away
- two or more players

AIM OF THE GAME

To win the most marbles

How to play

1. Each player puts an equal number of marbles around the ring so that they are evenly spaced.

2. The players takes turns to shoot their taws from the line, trying to knock the marbles off the ring.

3. Players win any marbles they knock off.

4. Players who don't manage to knock off any marbles must add their taws to those in the ring.

5. When the ring is empty, the player who has collected the most marbles is the winner.

Shoot out

What you need

- a circle about a metre (3 feet) in diameter
- two or more players

AIM OF THE GAME

To win the most marbles

How to play

1. Each player puts an equal number of marbles into the ring.

2. The players take turns to shoot their taws at the marbles from the edge of the ring (no fudging, please!)

3. If a player doesn't manage to hit a marble out of the ring, it's the next player's turn.

4. If a player hits a marble out of the ring and the taw goes out too, the player keeps the marble but it is the next person's turn.

5. If a player hits a marble out of the ring and the taw stays inside the ring, the player has another turn.

6. At the end of each turn, the player removes the taw.

7. When all the marbles have been shot from the ring, the player with the most marbles wins the game.

Bull's eye

What you need

* a circle about thirty centimetres (12 inches) in diameter
* two or more players

AIM OF THE GAME

To win the most marbles

How to play

1. Everyone puts an equal number of marbles into the centre of the ring.

2. Each player in turn stands at the edge of the ring and drops a taw from about waist— (or shoulder—) height.

3. If any marbles are knocked out of the ring, that player keeps them and removes the taw.

4. If no marbles are knocked from the ring, the player must add an extra marble to the centre.

5. The game continues until there are no marbles left in the ring.

6. The player with the most marbles is the winner

King of the Castle

What you need

* a circle about twenty centimetres (8 inches) in diameter
* a shooting line at least 1½ metres (4½ feet) away
* at least two players

To become the King of the Castle

How to play

1. To choose who will be King first, each player rolls a marble at the circle from behind the shooting line. The player whose marble goes closest to the circle, but not in it, is the King.

2. The King builds a castle in the centre of the ring by placing three marbles on the ground and then balancing a fourth on top of them as shown in the illustration.

3. The other players take turns to attack the castle by shooting a marble at it. Attacking players keep all marbles which are knocked out of the circle. If all the marbles are knocked out, the King must build another castle and the attacker has a second turn.

4. The King keeps any marbles, including the attacker's, which do not go outside the circle. If the attacking player misses the castle altogether, the King keeps that marble.

5. The King must rebuild the castle each time. When all the players have attacked, the next person has a turn at being King.

6. When everyone has had a turn, the player with the most marbles is King of the Castle.

Ring Taw

What you need

- an inner ring, or circle, about 30 centimetres (1 foot) in diameter, and an outer ring about 150 centimetres (about 5 feet) in diameter.

- two or more players

Aim of the game

To win the most marbles

How to play

1. Each player places two marbles in the inner ring.

2. Shooting from any position outside the large ring, the first player tries to knock one or more marbles from the small ring.

3. If successful, the player keeps those marbles and has another turn from where the taw came to rest. If not successful, the player leaves the taw where it rested until his turn comes round again.

4. If a taw is hit by another player, the owner must give a marble to that player.

5. When there are no marbles left in the ring, the player who has the most wins.

Hundreds

This game is for two players only

What you need

- a ring, about 20 centimetres (8 inches) in diameter

- a shooting line at least 1 metre (about 3 feet) away

Aim of the game

To be the first to score 100 points

How to play

1. Each player tries to shoot a marble into the circle. If both players are successful, they remove their marbles and try again. If both players continue to get their marbles into the circle, either make the circle smaller or move the shooting line further away.

2. When only one of the players gets a marble into the circle, that player scores 10 points and shoots again.

3. The player keeps shooting to improve his score until he misses or reaches 100 points.

4. If the player misses before reaching 100 points, it is the other player's turn.

5. The first player to reach 100 points wins.

Under Siege

What you need

* four circles, drawn one inside the other, with the largest about 60 centimetres (2 feet) in diameter

* two or more players

* ten marbles per player

AIM OF THE GAME

To win the most marbles by knocking them from the circles

How to play

1. The players each place four marbles in the inner circle, three into the next, two in the next and one in the outer circle.

2. Players take turns to shoot at marbles in the outer circle. They may shoot from anywhere they like, as long as they are at least two metres (about 6-7 feet) from the outer circle. Players keep any marbles they knock out, but must replace marbles dislodged from other circles.

3. Players who do not manage to knock out a marble must add an extra marble to the circle.

4. When the outer circle has no marbles left in it, the players move on to the next circle.

5. From now on, a player earns a bonus shot if:

* when attacking the 2nd circle, a marble is knocked out

* when attacking the 3rd circle, two marbles in a row are knocked out

* when attacking the inner circle, three marbles in a row are knocked out

6. Any player who does not manage to knock out a single marble is out of the game.

7. When the inner circle is empty, the player with the most marbles wins.

GAMES IN AN OPEN SPACE

Strike Three

What you need

* a playing area with enough room to move

* a starting line

* two players

AIM OF THE GAME

To chase the other player's marble and hit it three times in a row.

How to play

1. The players stand about two metres (6 feet) back from the starting line and throw a marble towards it. The person whose marble lands closest to the line without going over it has the first turn.

2. From the starting line, Player One shoots the taw in any direction.

3. Player Two tries to hit it.

4. If Player Two misses, it's Player One's turn to try and hit Player Two's marble. However, if Player Two hits Player One's marble, a second shot is allowed. If this is also successful, Player Two tries for a third strike. If all three shots hit the marble, Player Two keeps it.

5. The game restarts with the loser always having the first turn.

Lobs

As you need to dig a hole for this game, it cannot be played on a sealed surface such as concrete.

What you need

*   a shallow hole about eight centimetres (3 inches) in diameter
*   a shooting line at least one metre (3 feet) away
*   two players

AIM OF THE GAME

To lob as many marbles as possible into the hole

How to lob a marble

The player kneels or squats behind the shooting line with a marble in his cupped hands. By using a forward and upward movement, the player lobs the marble towards the hole. See opposite page.

How to play

1. As this game is played for keeps, everyone needs to agree on how many marbles are to be used by each player. Ten is usually about right.

2. To decide who starts the game, each player lobs a marble at the hole from behind the shooting line. The player whose marble goes closest, but not into, the hole has the first turn.

3. The first player lobs a marble at the hole. If it goes in, the player keeps the marble. If it does not, the other player claims it.

4. The players take turns at lobbing marbles until one of them exhausts his supply or the time agreed upon for the game is up. In that case, the player with the most marbles wins.

Marble Golf

As the name suggests, this game is a bit like golf and must also be played on a dirt surface. The playing area or course, which can have as many holes as you like, is more interesting if there are a few bumps and obstacles along the way — just like a real golf course.

What you need

*   a dirt playing area with at least four or five small holes
*   a starting line, about two metres (6 feet) from the first hole
*   two or more players

AIM OF THE GAME

To be the first player to complete the course

How to play

1. To decide who will start the game, the players stand behind the starting line and throw a marble towards the first hole. The player nearest the hole (or whose marble lands in it) goes first

2. Player One shoots the taw from behind the starting line to the first hole. If the taw goes in the hole (a hole-in-one), the player has another turn.

3. If the player did not shoot a hole-in-one, the taw remains where it landed until the next turn. During each turn, the player tries to get nearer the hole. When the taw finally lands in the hole, that hole is complete and the player moves to the next hole.

4. To hinder the progress of other players, a player is allowed to shoot at someone else's taw to try and knock it off course.

5. The first player to get around the course is the winner.

Forts

This game takes its name from olden times when enemies tried to storm fortified positions, known as forts.

What you need

*   two or more players sitting or kneeling at least two metres (six feet) apart

*   a taw plus four marbles per player to make a fort

Aim of the game

To destroy as many forts as possible

How to play

1. Draw a shooting line on the ground for each player, at least two metres (2½ yards) apart.

2. Each player builds a fort immediately behind his line by placing three marbles on the ground and balancing the fourth one on the top, as shown in the illustration for King of the Castle on page 72.

3. Players take turns to shoot at an opponent's fort. Anyone who knocks over a fort wins whatever marbles have been scattered. If this happens, the fort owner must rebuild or make a new fort with marbles from his stockpile. If a player misses a fort, the fort owner keeps the taw.

4. The player who has the most marbles after a set number of turns or after an agreed time, wins the game.

Shooting Gallery

What you need to make the gallery

- a cardboard shoebox or a series of hollow containers of varying shapes and sizes, such as small boxes, cardboard tubes from toilet rolls and disposable paper cups.

- a pencil or felt pen

- scissors

- masking or adhesive tape (if using containers)

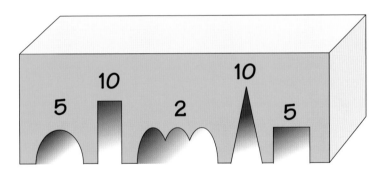

What to do

Either

1. With the pencil or felt pen draw a series of shapes (the targets), about three centimetres (1¼ inches) apart, along one side of the shoebox, as shown in the illustration. The shapes can be any design you like but should vary in size from not much bigger than a marble to about six centimetres (2½ inches) across.

2. Cut out the shapes carefully with the scissors.

3. Give each shape a number, with the smallest shapes having the highest numbers and largest the smallest.

Or

1. With the masking or adhesive tape join the various containers together in a row to form a series of targets, as shown in the illustration.

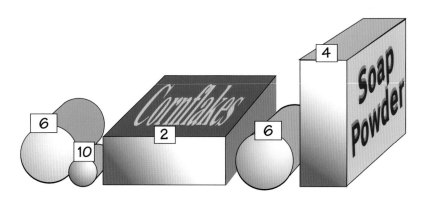

2. Give each container a number, with the smallest target having the highest numbers and the largest, the smallest. Either draw the numbers directly onto the tops of the containers or, if you prefer, write the numbers on small pieces of cardboard and then tape them upright onto the rim of each container.

To play the game you will need

✷ a shooting gallery

✷ at least two players

✷ a shooting line about two metres (6 feet) back from the gallery

AIM OF THE GAME

To shoot the highest score

How to play

1. To decide who will start the game, each player rolls a marble at the gallery from behind the shooting line. The player whose marble goes through the highest numbered target has the first turn.

2. The players take turns to shoot a marble at the targets. If the marble goes into the target shape the player scores the number marked on that target. The marble must stay inside the target shape to score.

3. After an agreed number of rounds the player with the highest score wins.

Business

In this game, players try to build their reserves by rolling marbles through the arches, which are in control of the banker.

What you need to make the arches

- ❋ a cardboard shoebox
- ❋ a pencil or felt pen
- ❋ a pair of scissors

What to do

1. Draw a series of arches with the pencil or pen along one side of the box as shown in the illustration. The arches should be at least twice the width of a marble.

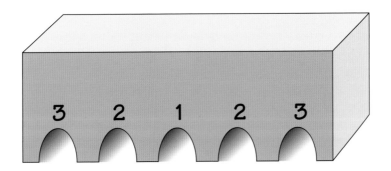

2. Cut out the arches carefully with the scissors.

3. Give each arch a number, with the arches in the centre having the lowest number and the ones on the outside having the highest, as shown in the illustration.

To play the game you will need

* a target arch box
* at least three players
* one player to be the banker
* a spare box or bag for the marble bank
* a shooting line about two metres (6 feet) back from the arches

AIM OF THE GAME

To win the most marbles from the banker

How to play

1. Players begin with an equal number of marbles. They give half of them to the banker who places them in the bank.

2. Player One rolls or shoots a marble at the arches from behind the shooting line.

3. If the marble goes through an arch, the banker gives the player the number of marbles shown above the arch.

4. If the marble does not go through an arch, the banker puts it in the bank.

5. After each round (or an agreed number of rounds), the first player becomes the banker.

6. When everyone has had a turn at being banker, the player with the most marbles is the winner.

Hopscotch

opscotch is probably the world's most widely-played game. It's called 'Marelles' in France, 'Infernaculo' in Spain, 'Templehupfen' in Germany and 'Ekaria dukaria' in India. The international hopscotch games in this book are just four of many.

BEFORE YOU BEGIN

The playing area

You can play hopscotch on any flat area, such as a playground, footpath or driveway. Scratch the hopscotch grid in the dirt with a stick or draw it on a hard surface with chalk. If you are allowed, use household paint or crayon for a longer lasting grid.

Taws

Since accurate throwing is essential for this game, the best taws are those which do not roll when they land. Try using one or two old keys tied together, a flat stone, a small ceramic tile or a tiny bag filled with sand. After a few throws you will find the taw that suits you.

General rules for hopscotch

1. The taw must land inside the correct square. If the taw lands on the line of the correct square the player must throw again.

2. Players are out if they:

   * hop in a square which has a taw in it

   * stand on a line

   * put their hands on a line, or in a square which has a taw in it, when trying to keep their balance

✴ change feet while hopping

✴ put two feet on the ground while hopping

Starting a game

To decide who will start the game, the players stand at the baseline with their backs to the grid and toss their taws over one shoulder. The player whose taw lands in the highest numbered square goes first.

GAMES TO PLAY

Ladder hopscotch

This game is harder than it looks! The rungs of the ladder are drawn so closely together that the players must hop sideways.

How to play

ONES

1. The player throws the taw into space one, hops over that space into space two, then three, four and so on, up to ten.

2. Landing on Home with both feet, the player turns around in one movement to land on both feet again then hops back to space two.

3. After picking up the taw from space one, the player hops over that space and out over the baseline.

TWOS, THREES, FOURS, ETC

1. The player throws the taw into space two, hops into space one, over space two and then into the other spaces as described for round one.

2. After picking up the taw from space two, the player must hop over it into space one, and then hop out.

LADDER

home
10
9
8
7
6
5
4
3
2
1

base line

3. The game continues in this way, with the taw being thrown into each space, including the Home square.

4. The first player to complete the grid is the winner.

If you want to prolong this game or make it harder, go through the entire sequence using the other foot.

VARIATIONS

✳ use other foot

✳ use only the even squares

✳ use only the odd squares

French hopscotch

How to play

GAME ONE

In this game the player is allowed only one hop in each square.

FRENCH

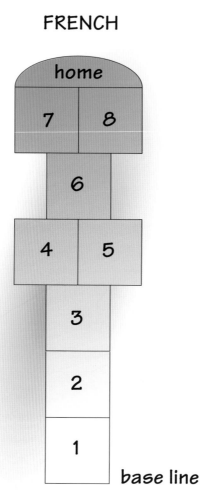

GAME ONE — LEVEL ONE

ONES

1. The player throws the taw into square one, hops over that square into square two, then into square three.

2.   After straddling squares four and five (legs apart with one foot in each square) the player hops into square six, straddles seven and eight and then turns around in one movement, straddling squares seven and eight as before.

3.   Repeating the sequence in the reverse order, the player hops back to square two, picks up the taw and then hops over square one across the baseline.

Twos

After throwing the taw into square two, the player hops into square one, over square two and into square three, and so on.

Threes

After throwing the taw into square three, the player hops into squares one and two, over square three to straddle four and five, and so on.

Fours (and fives, sevens and eights)

When the taw is in one of the straddled squares (four, five, seven or eight), the player must miss that square by hopping into the square beside it.

Sixes

When the taw is in square six the player, who is straddling squares four and five, straddle jumps directly into squares seven and eight.

Home

1.   The player throws the taw into Home and completes the sequence as normal, turning around in squares seven and eight.

2.   The player must then reach backwards and pick up the taw from Home, without touching a line, before returning to the baseline.

Game one — Level two

Repeat the entire sequence using the other foot.

GAME ONE — LEVEL THREE

This time use two feet (jumping). Squares four and five and seven and eight are still straddled.

GAME ONE — LEVEL FOUR

Same as Level three, with feet crossed at the ankles. When the player reaches squares four and five and seven and eight, the feet are uncrossed and the squares straddled normally.

GAME ONE — LEVEL FIVE

This level is by far the most difficult. The player must jump over an increasing number of squares, not just the square which has the taw. Before attempting Level five, make sure you are wearing shoes which support your ankles and have non-slip soles.

ONES

As for Level 1.

TWOS

1. After throwing the taw into square two, the player hops over squares one and two and into three before proceeding to squares seven and eight as before.

2. When returning to square three, the player picks up the taw from two, then hops over square two and into square one as usual.

THREES

After throwing the taw into square three, the player hops over squares one, two and three before proceeding as for twos.

FOURS, FIVES AND SO ON

The game continues in the same way with the player having to hop over an increasing number of squares each time. As the distance becomes greater, players may need to take a run up so that they can clear the squares more easily.

If you wish to advance to even harder levels, repeat the sequence for Level five using the other foot, both feet and then crossed feet.

GAME TWO

In this game, the player may take more than one hop in each square, but is allowed only one kick at the taw.

GAME TWO — LEVEL ONE

1. The player throws the taw into square one, hops over it to square two and turns around.

2. After hopping into square one the player uses the free foot to kick the taw out over the baseline before hopping out. If the taw lands short of the baseline, the next player has a turn.

3. If the kick is successful, the player throws the taw into the next square.

4. For squares four and five and seven and eight, the player straddles the squares (one foot in each square), then lifts the foot which is not in the taw square to kick the taw.

5. After completing all eight squares, the player moves to the opposite end of the grid. Standing outside Home to throw the taw, the player repeats the sequence in the reverse order. The player is not allowed to land in the home space and the taw must be kicked clear of it each time.

GAME TWO — LEVEL TWO

Repeat the game using the other foot.

GAME TWO — LEVELS THREE AND FOUR

Repeat the routine using both feet and then crossed feet.

Snail hopscotch

Called 'escargot' in France, two games can also be played using this grid.

SNAIL

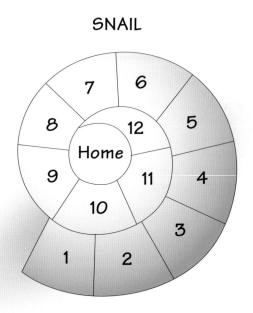

How to play

GAME ONE

For this game, which does not use a taw, players will need a piece of chalk.

1. The player hops through the grid, one hop only to each space, to Home.

2. The player may rest on Home with both feet before turning round and hopping back to the baseline.

3. When a player successfully hops to Home and back, that person's initials are chalked in any space chosen by the player, except Home.

4. From now on, the player may rest on both feet in that space, but no other player is allowed to hop into it. When players

come to any initialled space other than their own, they must hop over it.

5.   The game becomes harder as the spaces are initialled. When there is only one player left who can complete the grid, that person is the winner.

GAME TWO

1.   The first player throws a taw into space one, hops over it to space two, and then on to space twelve, taking only one hop in each space.

2.   The player may rest on Home with both feet before turning round, hopping back to space two, picking up the taw and hopping out over space one.

3.   Always standing at the baseline, the player throws the taw into a higher numbered space each time before hopping through the grid as already described. The player must always hop over the space which has the taw in it both coming and going.

4.   When the taw is in the Home space, the player picks it up while standing on one foot in space twelve, turns around in that space in one movement and then hops back to the baseline.

5.   The first player to complete the grid is the winner.

English hopscotch

How to play

GAME ONE

1.   The player throws the taw into square one, hops into that square, turns around (still on one foot) and uses the hopping foot to kick the taw back over the baseline. Any number of hops and kicks are allowed, but the taw must not land on the line and the player must not tread on a line or put the other foot on the ground.

2.   The player throws the taw into square two, hops to that square and repeats the process, moving to a higher numbered square each time.

ENGLISH

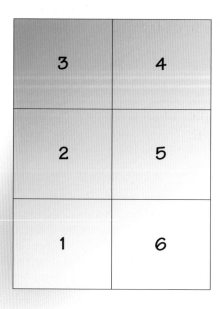

3.   The player who reaches square six first is the winner.

When all the players have had a turn hopping on one foot, the game may be repeated using the other foot, then both feet, then crossed feet.

GAME TWO

ONES

Holding the taw between the feet, the player jumps into square one, then square two and so on up to six. The player may take any number of jumps, but must not drop the taw or land on a line. On reaching square six, the player jumps out.

TWOS

Holding the taw between the feet as before, the player jumps over square one and into square two, then into three, four, and so on.

THREES, FOURS, FIVES AND SIXES

The player repeats the routine, jumping over a higher numbered square each time. The first player to complete round 6 is the winner.

American hopscotch

This is the most complex of all the hopscotch games which appear in this book and is perhaps the most interesting.

AMERICAN

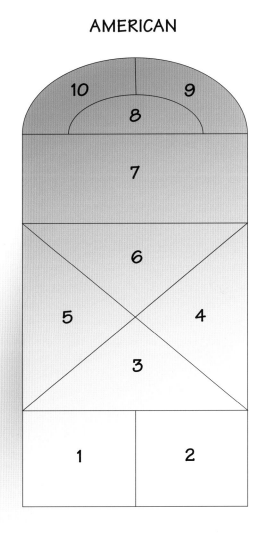

How to play

LEVEL ONE

ONES

1. Standing on one foot behind the baseline, the player throws the taw into square one and then hops into that square using the same foot.

2. Still on the same foot, the player kicks the taw out over the baseline before hopping out.

3. If the taw does not go out over the baseline in one kick, or the player breaks any of the normal hopscotch rules, it is the next player's turn.

TWOS

1. After throwing the taw into square two, the player hops into square one, then square two before kicking the taw out over the baseline as before.

2. The player now hops into square one, then out over the baseline.

THREES

1. After throwing the taw into triangle three, the player straddles squares one and two (one foot in each square), before hopping on one foot into triangle three.

2. The player now tries to kick the taw towards or beyond the baseline. If it stops in one of the other spaces without landing on a line the player may hop into that space and kick it out before hopping over the baseline as before. The player may take small hops within the space to get a better position before kicking the taw.

3. If the taw is kicked out over the baseline in one go, the player straddles squares one and two before hopping out.

FOURS

1. After throwing the taw into triangle four, the player goes through the routine as for threes and then hops into triangle four.

2. The return sequence is the same as for steps 2 and 3, as described in Threes, above.

FIVES

After throwing the taw into triangle five, the player proceeds as described in Fours, above.

SIXES

The routine now changes slightly.

1. The player throws the taw into triangle six, straddles spaces one and two, hops into space three and then straddles spaces four and five.

2. Landing on one foot, the player hops into triangle six and kicks the taw as usual before hopping out over the baseline, hopping and straddling in the same pattern as described in step 1.

SEVENS

1. After throwing the taw into rectangle seven, the player follows the same routine as for Sixes, then jumps with both feet into the rectangle.

2. The player may shuffle about the rectangle, using one or both feet to reposition the taw before kicking it as usual, using the same pattern of hopping and straddling to the baseline as described before.

EIGHTS

1. After throwing the taw into semi-circle eight, the player follows the same routine as for Sevens, before hopping on one foot into space eight.

2. The player then kicks the taw as usual, following the same pattern as previously described.

NINES

There is now another change to the routine.

1. After throwing the taw into the arc marked nine, the player follows the same routine to space eight.

2. While balancing on one foot in space eight the player uses one hand to pick up the taw before returning to the base line, carrying the taw and using the same straddling and hopping pattern as before.

TENS

1. After throwing the taw into the arc marked ten, the player follows the usual routine, but this time hops on one foot from space eight into space nine.

2. Balancing carefully, the player picks up the taw and returns to the baseline, following the same pattern as before.

ELEVENS

Place the taw to one side, as it is no longer needed.

1. Following the same routine as before, the player hops into space eight.

2. From space eight the player straddles spaces nine and ten, before turning around in one movement to face the opposite direction, straddling the same squares.

3. The player then hops on one foot into space eight before returning to the baseline in the usual way.

LEVEL TWO

Repeat the entire sequence using the other foot.

LEVEL THREE

This time jump through the routine using two feet, except in the spaces which are normally straddled.

LEVEL FOUR

This is the same as Level three, except the feet are crossed at the ankles. When the player reaches spaces which are usually straddled, the feet are uncrossed and the spaces straddled in the normal way.